WHAT'S YOUR SPORT? GOLF

WHAT'S YOUR SPORT?

GOLF

HOWARD CLARK
WITH MITCHELL PLATTS

PARTRIDGE PRESS

LONDON · NEW YORK · TORONTO · SYDNEY · AUCKLAND

TRANSWORLD
PUBLISHERS LTD
61-63 Uxbridge Road,
London W5 5SA
TRANSWORLD
PUBLISHERS
(AUSTRALIA) PTY LTD
15-23 Helles Avenue,
Moorebank NSW 2170
TRANSWORLD
PUBLISHERS (NZ) LTD
Cnr Moselle and
Waipareira Aves,
Henderson, Auckland
Published 1989 by
Partridge Press
a division of Transworld
Publishers Ltd
Copyright © Howard
Clark 1989

British Library
Cataloguing in
Publication Data
Clark, Howard
    What's your sport: golf.
    1. Golf
    I, Title   II. Platts,
Mitchell
    796.352

    ISBN 1-85225–057–7

Printed in Great Britain
by Mackays of Chatham
PLC, Letchworth

Designed by Graham
Mitchener
Illustrations Chris Lyon
All photographs by
Lawrence Levy except:
14, 27, 29 Phil Sheldon; 19,
32 Philip Thomas; 23 Jan
Traylen, 25 S&G, 37
Dunlop/Slazenger

CONTENTS

INTRODUCTION

When I started playing golf, at the age of ten, I didn't realise quite how far the game would take me. It has provided me, personally, with a lifestyle I would not have been able to attain in any other business unless I had been extraordinarily fortunate. I might have become a stockbroker or reached the peak of a sales career, but the chances are that would not have happened.

Yet what is most important is that when I started out I only wanted to play for fun. I'm sure my father, Keith, who was himself a scratch handicap golfer, had ideas of me playing better than him. I came from an all-round golfing background because my mother, too, played a fair game. So clearly there was something in the chemistry! And as a schoolboy in short trousers, my one true love was the game of golf.

I think that for anybody the important thing about breaking into golf is not to look too far ahead. It is more likely than not that there will not be a spectacular amateur career – or a lucrative professional life – in the future. Yet everybody who picks up a golf club can be certain of gaining something from the game: simply look at the pleasure it can provide. Golf takes you out into the fresh air, taking you away from the town or city, and it gives you the opportunity to pit your skills, competitive or otherwise, against an opponent with whom you are usually fairly handicapped.

The important thing about breaking into golf is not to look too far ahead

Opposite:
Howard Clark willing
the ball into the
hole.

That is the beauty of golf. It is a game for the young and the old, men and women, boys and girls, and a game which offers outdoor exercise and outstanding entertainment. When you are at school it provides a pastime for holidays and weekend and I know that parents are delighted in this day and age to know that their children are off the streets enjoying life on the fairways. And, should you become a business person, those same fairways can provide a congenial setting for discussing commercial transactions.

I've been fortunate, especially since I started playing as a professional, in meeting a number of fine people who have been able to help me in my career. And I honestly do not believe that there are many sports which can run close to golf in terms of generating new friends. Of course, I am one of the lucky ones because I can also see the world and derive a lot of pleasure from following my occupation.

You, too, can extract as much fun and pleasure from the game, and meet as many people as you wish, by taking up golf as a hobby. It is never too late to learn and never too late to get a sense of achievement from hitting, say, a five iron 168 yards to two feet from the pin. You don't have to be a professional to do that or, for that matter, to hole in one.

What it amounts to is having pride in your own performance, whether it is in breaking 100 for the first time or in stringing together a succession of par figures. Golf, you see, consistently stretches you into achieving goals which you might have believed to be unreachable.

This is true at all levels of the game. When you're starting out, and you meticulously keep that first scorecard, you must not become despondent because it has taken you 139 shots to play 18 holes when Jack Nicklaus has just shot 65 round Augusta. You must think (and Jack will be doing the same even after a score such as that) of where you might have saved shots. You must think how you are going to turn that 139 into a 129 the next week. You must think of the day when you are going to break 100 . . . then 90 . . .

then 80. That is the trick. Even now, for a professional such as myself, the secret is how to shave off another shot per round.

NEW GOALS

It is impossible to say, after a dozen rounds or so, that you are now a golfer; that you have learnt to play and that there is nothing more to it. You must set yourself new goals all the time, especially if you are an aspiring youngster dedicated to carving out a career in the game.

This is what I have done. These are the steps up the ladder that professional golfers have been compelled to take. The likes of Nick Faldo and Sandy Lyle, Severiano Ballesteros and Bernhard Langer, Ian Woosnam and myself, and many more besides, all had to learn from scratch. For us now, of course, golf is a business, but it is also important to enjoy it even if the wind is howling and the rain is slanting across the fairways.

There is no limit to what you can get out of golf. The secret is to enjoy every minute: to be delighted by your high points and to have the strength of character to accommodate the lows. I hope that this book will provide a guideline to how to go about making the game of golf a pleasurable experience. It is that to millions of people around the world today, which is testimony enough to the game's extraordinary magnetic qualities.

HOWARD CLARK

1 HOW TO GET GOING

The door is wide open to anybody who wants to take up the game of golf. The game's booming popularity has generated huge interest, so that today more and more youngsters are encouraged to play. You can start tomorrow, simply by acquiring a club and a ball, but my immediate advice, whatever your age, is to seek information from the professional at your local golf club.

Sandy Lyle struck his first shot at the age of three. I am reliably informed that the ball travelled more than 60 yards even though Sandy was wearing a pair of wellington boots! Sandy, of course, was fortunate in that his father was the professional at the Hawkstone Park Club in Shropshire. Sandy does possess a rare talent, but it is still a bonus if you start young.

With me it happened that my father, who played off scratch for many years, was competing in a friendly match. Because I was being a bit of a pest, he gave me a two iron and a ball and told me to go over to the side of the fairway. It was early evening and there was nobody, apart from us, on the course. I'm sure he never thought that I would connect, let alone hit the ball a reasonable distance. In fact with my first swing the ball sailed some 80 yards through the air and over the head of my astonished father! I was nine years old at the time.

I immediately fell head over heels in love with

golf. It is that kind of sport. There are men and women from other sports who refuse to take a stab at golf because they fear they will become hooked on the game. I have certainly channelled all my energies into the sport. And I honestly believe **It is easier to make golf your pastime** it is easier to make golf YOUR pastime **today than it was twenty years ago** pastime today than it was twenty years ago when I started out.

The attitude towards golf has changed a great deal. When I was at school even archery lessons were available, but there was no place for golf in the sports programme. I could never fathom that one out. It seemed to me that it might be pretty dangerous to practise archery, despite professional supervision, whereas golf is the kind of sport that would have fitted in safely and easily between classroom lessons. Sadly, it reached the point where my desire to play golf was so strong that I was driven away from the school.

THE GOLF FOUNDATION

I would doubt whether that would happen anywhere in the country today. Moreover, if you are fortunate enough to attend a school which has links with the Golf Foundation Coaching Scheme for Schools and Junior Groups then you can apply to enrol with them.

The Golf Foundation is the national body responsible for the promotion and development of junior golf. It was founded in 1952 – two years before I was born – with the specific aims of introducing more young people to the sport and developing their skills and enjoyment of the game. Throughout its history the Golf Foundation has steadfastly pursued these aims, with the result that thousands of junior golfers have benefited from its work. The responsibilities of the Golf Foundation include all aspects of the development of a junior golfer, and ensuring that young people's interest in the game is sustained through to the adult ranks.

The significance of the Golf Foundation in promoting junior golf can be easily appreciated. In 1972 the Golf Foundation Team Championship

for Schools was established; there was an entry of 112 teams. Today more than 1000 schools compete annually. The importance of this event is in providing intense competition under championship conditions. It is certainly true that many Team Championship competitors have progressed to international fame. Paul Way, the Ryder Cup player and former PGA champion, together with Michael McLean, who won the Cacharel Under-25 Championship in 1983, won the Team Championship for Hugh Christie School, Tonbridge, in 1980.

Opposite:
Ian Woosnam has been riding the crest of a wave in recent years

In association with the Professional Golfers' Association, the Golf Foundation recently relaunched the Coaching Award Scheme for school teachers. This is designed to qualify teachers to organise golf as a school sport, arrange competitions and teach the rudiments of the game in restricted conditions. The teacher who is successful in the coaching course, which covers safety, ball flight laws, equipment, the set-up, the swing, the short game, causes and cures of faults, competitive situations, and rules and etiquette, will then be able to link up with the PGA professional currently giving Golf Foundation coaching.

The importance of golf in schools is in providing sufficient experience of the game for youngsters to be able to decide early on whether or not they wish to channel their energies towards golf rather than another sport. Moreover, it will bring them into early contact with the rules of golf and, perhaps more importantly, with golfing etiquette. Matters of golfing courtesy are best learnt at an early stage. When you come to approach a golf club for membership, there is more likelihood of you being accepted if it is known that you have studied the etiquette of the game. You will be expected to dress well, and you will be expected to be aware of such things as calling through the players behind you should you be looking for a 'lost' ball.

To learn such fundamentals might seem incidental to some, but I cannot stress too much how invaluable it is to get a sound footing in the game. It is a sport which demands immense concentration, so it is imperative that you do not talk when your opponent is executing a shot or distract him in any way. It is a game which also demands tremendous common sense. Golf clubs, and balls for that matter, are dangerous. It is all too easy to squirt the ball at a sharp angle

or for a player to take a practice swing and strike you a cruel blow. Finally, golf is a game which has evolved under the banner of fair play, and if you put an incorrect figure on your scorecard you will gain nothing, as you will be cheating not only your opponent but also yourself.

Top professionals
like Bernard
Gallacher can
provide expert
tuition

The scorecard of a typical course

COMPETITION							DATE							Handicaps	Strokes Received
PLAYER A															
PLAYER B															
Marker's Score	Hole	Yards	Par	Stroke Index	A	B	Result or Points	Marker's Score	Hole	Yards	Par	Stroke Index	A	B	Result or Points
	· 1	337	4	15					10	317	4	14			
	2	370	4	11					11	501	5	4			
	3	418	4	3					12	149	3	18			
	4	412	4	9					13	327	4	12			
	5	197	3	13					14	155	3	16			
	6	487	5	1					15	466	4	2			
	7	398	4	7					16	384	4	8			
	8	183	3	17					17	455	4	6			
	9	522	5	5					18	396	4	10			
	OUT	3324	36						IN	3150	35				
									OUT	3324	36				
									TOTAL	6474	71				
											H'CAP				
											NET				

Marker's Signature . . . .

Player's Signature . . . .

N.B. THE MARKER IS RESPONSIBLE FOR RECORDING THE GROSS SCORE AT EACH HOLE.

S.S.S.71

On the subject of the scorecard, this will show you the distance for each hole, usually in yards (although metric measurements are becoming more common), as well as the par for each hole, which indicates the score that a scratch handicap golfer is expected to make at a hole. Although there can be variations, most 18-hole courses will have an even balance of four long holes, or par fives, which measure in excess of 476 yards, four short holes, or par threes, which measure up to 245 yards, and ten par fours. These are generally laid out in two loops of nine.

Each hole begins from a teeing ground, which is usually an elevated oblong of prepared turf. This is where you can tee the ball up on a small peg made of wood or plastic. You are allowed to practice swings, but every time you swing the club with the intention of hitting the ball counts as a stroke, so even if you miss it must still be added to your score for that hole. You play from a tee to a green, which is a manicured surface on which you putt out into a hole measuring 4 ¼ inches, but there are many obstacles, such as bunkers, rough, trees and water, to overcome on the way. The idea is to remain on the fairway at par fours and fives, since this is a cut area from which it is far easier to play a shot. At par threes, some of which can measure as little as 100 yards, the intention is to hit the ball straight from the tee on to the green. If you should be so fortunate as to hit the ball straight into the hole from the tee (and the odds against this have been calculated as 40,000 to 1), then this is known as a hole in one or an ace.

HANDICAP

The progress that you make can be gauged by your handicap. Initially you will not have one, and you cannot obtain one until you become a member of a club. The maximum handicap for a man is 28 and for a woman it is 36. Handicaps are designed to bring parity to the scores of good and not so good players. For example, take a course with a par of 72 and three players with handicaps of 2, 12 and 28. The player off 2 shoots a 74, but with his handicap deducted his 'net' score is 72. The 12-handicapper has an 84, less 12, so that he too scores 72. The player off 28 takes 100, less his allowance, so that once again 72 has been scored. So the three players have tied. It will not always work out that equally, of course, but the basic premise of the game is enjoyment and with a good handicap system, as operated in this country, it is always possible to have a fairly evenly balanced game.

The fact that golfers of varying skills and abilities can play one another is one of the great attractions of the game. The sport is becoming increasingly popular, and more courses will have to be developed to cope with demand as we approach the twenty-first century. Schools will inevitably play an increasingly influential role, and if you have leanings towards the game, it is best to learn all you can about the rudiments of golf while still of school age.

I started out in golf by caddying for my father. At that stage this was mainly to get me out of the house and to keep me away from anything I should not be doing out of school time. I learned by watching him, and other amateur golfers, play in Leeds and District matches and Yorkshire county matches. As with anything else, it was first a question of learning the basics. You soon discover that the game is not simple, and you don't just hit a driver and then walk down to the fairway where a marker states that it is a five iron from there to the green. You must learn to master the art of distance and flight, and to do so you must have the desire and the determination to overcome the disappointments that will certainly come your way.

The object of this book, however, is not to instruct you on how to grip the club or how to swing it. It is to provide you with the information on how to go about getting into the game and how best to ensure that you are prepared to take the good with the bad, the birdies with the bogies. If you are a youngster and the school you attend is not involved in the Golf Foundation Coaching Scheme, or if you are an adult wishing to begin playing the game, then the first step is to approach your local club. The secretary of the club, which will usually have memberships in varying categories from junior to mid-week to full, will provide you with an application form to join. (I must warn you at this point that some waiting lists may seem longer than the Amazon river!)

THE CLUB PROFESSIONAL

It is equally important to see the local club professional. He can tell you much more about the cost of being kitted out to play the game. This can be relatively inexpensive initially, for just a few clubs will be enough until you decide whether or not you want to pursue the sport, although when it comes to purchasing a full set of high-class clubs you will have to think in terms of between £500 and £1000. But do not allow that figure to dampen your spirits. Remember that those clubs will be your property for life if you treat them well, and that you can derive enjoyment from them once, twice, maybe three times

each week. Moreover, the local professional usually has a few 'specials' up his sleeve, so you can always hunt for a set that will suit your pocket.

If you are a youngster, and your parents are not involved in golf, then it is true that you may find it somewhat difficult to walk into a professional's shop with the intention of getting fully kitted out for the game. But you should try to help yourself. I am sure that most parents would be pleased to see their sons and daughters become fascinated by the game of golf, if only because if provides them with an interest during the school holidays. Far better that they be enjoying themselves on the golf course than getting up to mischief somewhere else. So urge your parents to come along with you to talk to the professional.

If you like watching golf on television, I am sure that you are going to like it even more when you get out on the course. Recently it seems to have been hammered into us that snooker is becoming more popular than golf. But I believe that this may be misleading, because it is relatively easy to play a frame of snooker in the lunch hour, whereas golf is a lot more time-consuming. In other words, you will need to have more get up and go to become a golfer.

I accept that golf does have the reputation of consisting of exclusive clubs which may sometimes seem as impenetrable as Fort Knox. But I promise you that it is possible to go along to the majority and have your questions answered. For instance, I would have no hesitation in saying that you would be welcomed at a club such as Wentworth where the professional, Bernard Gallacher, or one of his assistants, would do everything possible to help you; you will not be turned away. Just remember to help yourself by dressing well and being polite.

All you need initially is one lesson. This might last only for thirty minutes, but you will find out in that time whether or not you are going to enjoy golf. Then, if you do, you can start thinking about buying some equipment, but not too much at first, in case you change your mind (although I think that unlikely once you've been hooked). It is imperative that you seek professional tuition from the start. That is half the battle. Starting out with a good grip is one of the secrets of the game.

Starting out with a good grip is one of the secrets of the game

You could progress by going on special golfing holidays designed to improve your game. These are marshalled by former touring professionals such as John Garner, David Huish and Brian Waites. They offer, say, a group of twenty or thirty a week in Spain or Portugal with expert tuition. It is money well spent – if you can afford it!

Driving ranges are a very good idea, because there is no limit to how much time you can spend there. And you don't have to be a club member. They are usually undercover so you can play in any conditions, rain or shine, day or night, and they provide a good method of practising what you are being taught. However, I would not recommend you going to a driving range and hacking balls here, there and everywhere without having first learnt some of the

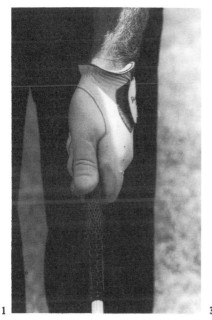

1

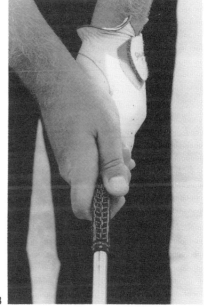

2

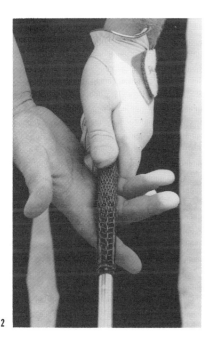

3

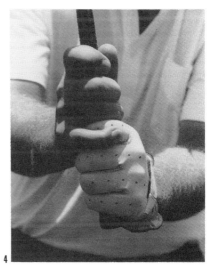

4

The first thing in
golf is to get a grip!
This sequence
shows the
overlapping, or
Vardon, grip

21

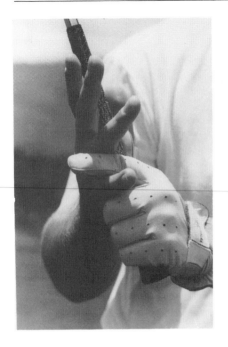

Left (top and bottom): The interlocking grip favoured by Jack Nicklaus

Right (top): The baseball grip (bottom): The overlapping, or Vardon, grip

fundamental principles of the game.

Honing the swing at the 1988 Open Championship

If you ignore this advice, then it is more than likely that you will develop a bad swing, unless you are an absolute natural at the game. There *are* some of those about, but they are rare pearls indeed. Even so, I'm sure it is possible to watch golfers of the calibre of Seve Ballesteros and Greg Norman, and even a few of the lesser-known players, and pick up some helpful thoughts on your swing. Nevertheless, I am of the opinion that the majority of newcomers to the sport will not help themselves if they attempt to 'steal' their game from one of the superstars. What might be good for Ballesteros might not necessarily suit you. The best advice is to let the touring professionals be your inspiration, and let the club professionals be your guiding light.

2 GOLFING ETIQUETTE

There is no more important subject within the game of golf than etiquette. Bobby Jones, arguably the greatest golfer that ever lived, once wrote 'Golf, in my view, is the most rewarding of all games because it possesses a very definite value as a moulder or developer of character. The golfer very soon is made to realise that his most immediate and perhaps his most potent adversary is himself.'

There are many things that make a champion. Henry Cotton, with whom I worked in the 1970s, once pointed out to me the importance of taking things step by step. He, perhaps more than anybody else, knew exactly what was required to mould your game character. Henry was strong on desire: he explained how this had to be an obsession, a passion. He expressed, too, the need to understand your swing and the will to practise. The golfer must learn to concentrate, acquire co-ordination and obtain emotional control. In other words, he must be able to take both the knocks and the good breaks with equanimity.

Henry campaigned with the objective that young people entering the sport would not only understand all that was required of them, but also appreciate how the game could help them in life. He emphasised his four rules of life for any champion, and they are worth remembering.

Henry said: 'Live for something other than yourself. If you think only of yourself you will find thou-

sands of reasons for being unhappy, you will never have had the treatment which you thought you deserved and you will never have done all you wanted to do or should have done . . . Build up a present of which you can be proud. Whoever lives for a purpose . . . forgets his own troubles and worries.

Act, instead of lamenting the absurdities of this world. We must try to transform our own small lot . . . . To do your own job well and become a master at it is not always easy, but you will find happiness in working hard and making a success of your job, whatever it might be.

You must believe in the power of your own will. I do not believe that the future is completely predetermined. Whoever has the courage and strength of will can, to a certain extent, control his destiny . . . . Laziness and cowardice are weaknesses, work and courage are acts of will. And strength of purpose is perhaps the queen of virtues.

Never deceive. Faithfulness is perhaps as valuable as strength of purpose. It is not an easy virtue. You must be true to your promises, to your contract, to others and to yourself.

These rules are very harsh, but you must add to them a sense of humour – it will enable you to smile at yourself, and with others.'

These thoughts apply equally to life in general and the game of golf in particular. To have the **Every golfer is his own referee**   desire to win is important, but to have the knowledge of how to win, and more importantly how to lose, is even more important. From the very first moment you strike a golf ball it is important that you realise that the game is not only a tremendous test of one's character but also of one's honesty. Golf is regarded as the most honourable of sports, for the very simple reason that every golfer is his own referee. If you cheat at golf, you are cheating only yourself. This you must learn right from the start, in company with all that is required of you in terms of golfing etiquette. Mastering golfing etiquette is as important as mastering the game itself.

COURTESY

In the first instance, let us say that we are going to have a game of golf and we talk on the phone with our opponent or opponents and decide on a time to play. If we agree on 9 o'clock, then it is imperative for each one of us to make sure that we are on the first tee and ready to play at 9 o'clock sharp. Many clubs have a starting time list, especially for the weekend, and so failure to adhere to the times that we set ourselves will probably serve to punish us, for we may have to wait an hour or two before being able to tee off; but it will also spoil the game for other players.

From the moment that we tee off it is important to show courtesy not only to the players with whom we are competing but also those in front and behind us. Do not hit a golf ball if it would appear that you can send it far enough to disturb those players in front. And if you should lose a ball, then it is important to call those players through who are playing behind you.

Golf is a game from which we can derive great pleasure, and we will get more out of it if we play

Courtesy is required on a crowded course

smartly round the course. In some countries, especially in America, the five-hour round for amateurs has become the norm. If you want to spend the entire day talking stocks and shares on the golf course, then perhaps this is OK for you. But I believe that most people play golf principally for the enjoyment of the game, and so it is essential to get round the course in a reasonable time in order to allow other competitors to do the same.

However, we must not go so fast as to neglect those things that are important to ensure that everybody enjoys the same facilities. Remember, if you hit the ball into a bunker it is your duty to smooth out all the footprints and the club marks that you have made during your foray into the sand. Some people think that a quick shake with the sole of the foot is sufficient. It is not. The golf club where you play will probably have rakes around most bunkers and you should use these to smooth out the sand; if not, then take your time and do the job with your golf club. If you fail to do so and the player behind you is two down with two to play, hits his ball into the bunker and finishes in the footprint which you left, then it is likely that you will have to face a minor contretemps in the clubhouse when he arrives. So do make sure that this doesn't happen.

You should also remember to replace all the divots that you uproot as you move from tee to green. When you play a shot firmly, and especially with clubs like the wedge or eight or nine iron, it is inevitable that you will cut into the turf. The slice of turf that you take out should be neatly replaced from where it came and pushed down lightly with the sole of your shoe. By doing this you will give the grass an excellent chance of recovering. Often you will see several divots lying here and there on fairways, and that is not always the fault of the player: sometimes birds turn them over in search of worms. If you do have the time then it is not a bad idea to replace some of these divots as you go along, simply because that will help your golf course to remain in the best of conditions.

GREENS

On reaching the green, remember never to take your trolley (if you are pulling one) on to the green or anywhere close to it, and never to drop your bag of clubs on the green. If you are pulling a trolley, try to take it round the outside of a line which includes the bunkers. In that way you will not damage the grass between bunkers and green. I know that today it is mainly the wide-wheeled trollies that are used, and these are much better, but at the same time if we remember from the start that we want to protect our course in every possible way, then keeping trollies off it is certainly one way in which we can do that.

When you take the flag from the hole, do so with care. It is the job of the greenkeeper to cut the hole in such a way that it will always be square and sharp so that the ball when striking the side of the hole will drop into it. What we do not want to see is players lifting the flag out too hurriedly so that they perhaps just pull an edge out of the side of the hole. Believe me, it is easily done, so take your time and ensure that you don't do any damage in this department.

It is important to look after the greens at all times

On the greens it is imperative too that you walk with care. It is very easy to scuff the turf with your golf spikes. If you do so by mistake then try to smooth them out gently, perhaps by tapping your putter softly down on top of the scuff marks that you have made. The damage that you are most likely to cause the greens occurs when the ball lands on the putting surface and causes a pitch mark. This must be repaired immediately. If it is not then I can assure you that it will take the greenkeeper some time to get that small hole once again looking like the rest of the green. Imagine how it would look if a hundred golfers played during one day and not one of them repaired the pitch mark. It is all too easy to blame the greenkeeper, but if the members of the club help him by repairing their pitch marks then I assure you it will be most beneficial to you, the player. Repairing a pitch mark is an art form. Don't just stick a tee peg in behind it and tap it down with your foot. Think about what you are doing, try to learn from a professional and devote your time and attention to the matter. It is quite likely, if your game is not in good shape, that you will go to the local pro and ask him for a lesson. Why not spend a couple of minutes with him finding out how best to repair a pitch mark? If you get it right from the start then you will always know how to do it, and you will always be a friend to your greenkeeper.

From the time we tee off to the time we putt out, it is also important that we realise what is required of us as opponents. It is always best to stand to the side of your playing partner and not to the front or directly behind. That, of course, is obvious when we are talking about driving the ball or hitting a five-iron shot of 160 yards, but it is also important when we are on the greens. It is all too easy for you to be distracted when putting by an opponent, should he be standing in front of or behind you. So make sure, if you want to receive help from your opponents, that you help them by following this golden rule.

Keeping quiet might seem obvious advice, but I assure you that there are still a number of people who rustle or make noises when others are playing shots. This is something that we must never do, because it is extremely annoying to a player who is about to hit. Until it has happened to you, you will perhaps not realise how a noise on your backswing or when you are standing over a putt can affect the shot or stroke. Be aware of this at all times, and remember when you are on a green that somebody else in another match could be teeing off on a nearby hole. So even if you are talking to your opponent, do so quietly and in a manner that will not disturb other players on the course.

Another point concerning talking on the golf course is not to have a long conversation after you have holed out in the middle of the green. The players behind you are waiting to get on with it, and if they see you standing there holding the flag then it is pretty obvious that they will get extremely upset. So put the flag back into the hole smartly and correctly and get off the green before you chat about how or why you came to win or lose that hole.

THE CLUBHOUSE

You should now have a good idea about how to get round a golf course, so we shall move on to clubhouse etiquette. The first thing that you should recognise is that your shoes are probably covered in grass or mud, and outside the clubhouse there is usually a place where you can clean your shoes. Do so, because if you don't you will take that mud and grass into the dressing room. Once inside you will probably take a shower, and after that it is far better to walk across a floor that is not splattered with mud or grass. Some clubs make a point of stressing how important it is to change your shoes and golfing gear in the clubhouse rather than outside. I agree with this, but I think it is generally realised now that it is best to put your clubs straight back into the car and *lock up*. Very many clubs are stolen each year from golf club car parks and this is usually done between rounds or when players have just returned to the clubhouse after a round and gone

in to change. So I would recommend that on leaving the last green you take your clubs to the car, lock them up, go to the shoe cleaner and then go into the club.

Opposite:
It is important to know what the correct dress is in a golf club

The question of the correct dress in a golf club is a dynamic subject. Many people believe that they should be allowed to wear whatever they want when they go into the club. However, let me tell you that the jacket and tie remains obligatory in many clubs, even in the United States where casual wear is more prevalent, so it is better that you recognise this from the start. In some clubs there will be a spike bar where you can walk straight in, order a drink or a sandwich and have a chat before leaving to go home. This, of course, is quite acceptable and a very good idea indeed, but if you are going into the club to stay and maybe have some lunch, then you will have to dress properly. Jeans are not appropriate attire for golf clubs. Some permit polo necks, but what you really have to do is from the moment you become a member of the club, check with them what is required of you in terms of dress. In this way all members will conform to the same standards, and you as an individual will never be embarrassed.

It is true that some clubs are relaxing their rules on dress, and if this is the case then be aware of what your own club requires. Golf is a noble game and so if we as individuals help to keep our standard of dress and our knowledge of etiquette high, then that will ensure the game's continuing good reputation.

3 EQUIPMENT

The first thing to remember about equipment is that no one knows better than your local professional. A full set of golf clubs consists of fourteen, which is the maximum you are allowed to carry in the bag under the rules of the game. To most people this means four woods – usually driver, three, four, and five – nine irons (numbered three to nine then pitching wedge and sand wedge) and a putter. Your local professional, however, should initially set out the minimum requirement. A short set consisting of a couple of woods, maybe a two and a four or a three and a five, and six irons (three, five, seven, nine, pitching wedge and sand wedge) should be sufficient. A lot of short sets contain only one wedge, but I think this is one area where it is important to be fully equipped. You will find more gorse bushes and bunkers than you will care to remember in those early 'happy hacking' days, so it is best to carry the artillery with which to escape. Two wedges will give you the edge over another newcomer to the game.

WOODS

When I was learning to play, we had only wooden woods. Now we have the metal wood, which is certainly a contradiction in terms. The metal woods unquestionably have a longer life span. Moreover, many of them are very good and there is an increasing selection from which to choose. On the other

Opposite:
The golf bag carries much more than just the golf clubs

Opposite:
Close-up of woods
and irons

hand, many professionals still prefer the 'old-fashioned' woods. We might have seen the end of the hickory shafts – steel, graphite and goodness knows what other substances have come along to replace them – but I doubt whether we will ever see the day when the metal wood completely takes over from a good old piece of persimmon. Yet it is important to remember that if you purchase wooden ones then it is absolutely vital that you look after them. Leave them to dry in the boot of the car with the head covers on and they might never be the same again. Swelling will occur and the wood will push away from the insert (basically the hitting area) – so do beware.

To return to basics, we can now be agreed that clubs are divided into two types – woods and irons. You will hear a number one wood almost always referred to as a driver. Yet it is becoming increasingly noticeable that the names brassie (two wood) and spoon (three wood) are disappearing. This is perhaps understandable in that the trend in recent years has been to extend the number of woods that we can carry in the bag so that apart from the four and the five some manufacturers even produce six and seven woods. There is also a selection of bafflers, which are woods with ridges on the sole of the club head which help it to pass through the rough, so enabling the golfer to get a better hit from a bad lie. (The word baffler unquestionably stems from the word 'baffy' which was the equivalent of today's number four wood.) It is not a bad club for a long-handicapped amateur or a newcomer to carry.

The numbers supposedly tell us the loft of each **Every manufacturer has his own** club. In fact, they most certainly do **particular loft selection for clubs** not in the case of woods and metal woods. The fact is that every manufacturer has his own loft selection, so the four wood of one could have a loft similar to the five wood of another. This is unlikely to bother you if you are just starting; but in time it will, because you will want a selection of clubs which enable you to hit any distance with a full

swing. In essence, the driver will hit the ball lower than a three wood, and a three wood will hit it lower than a five wood. With the trajectory being different it is obvious that a driver will hit the ball further than a three wood. When you start out I am convinced that you will find it easier to hit a three wood, which is why I would recommend that you save your money for other things and initially ignore purchasing a driver.

IRONS

You will more easily notice the importance of grading clubs when you start to hit with your irons. Most professionals carry a one iron and some a two, in preference to one or two of the woods, but since these have hardly any loft at all it is best to forget all about them when you are starting out. As we go through from the three iron to the nine iron, each club has a greater degree of loft. The difference between each boils down to a hitting distance of ten yards.

All this might suggest that the game is very easy. You are 120 yards from the hole so you take your eight iron; at 140 yards out it is obviously a six iron; for a shot of 160 yards, a four iron. Forget it. Apart from allowing for the elements – a strong wind can make a club difference of three or four – there is a skill to be learned in stopping the ball on the green or in letting it pitch and run up towards the hole. This will all take a long time, and it is not for me to go into detail here. What I would stress is that players such as Seve Ballesteros did not go down to the local club, buy fourteen clubs and march out on to the golf course. He began his golfing life with a single rusty old club. What is interesting is that he learned to shape a variety of shots with that one club. So you will in fact benefit from having a short set, because you will need to make the five do the work of a four or a six. That is part of the learning process. Improvisation will also help to swell your enjoyment of the game.

The wedge and the sand wedge have extreme degrees of loft. You will learn to use both clubs for a

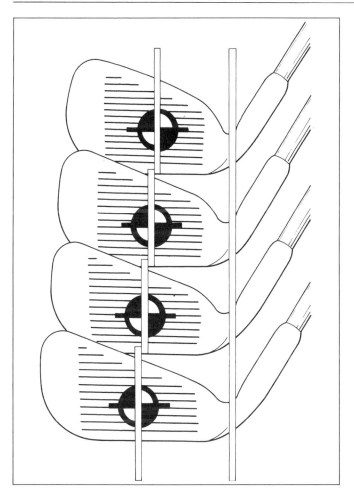

The shorter the iron, the shorter the distance between the sweet spot and the heel of the club. From top to bottom, the 9, 7, 5 and 2 irons

Below:
The full range of irons. As the irons get shorter, so the degree of loft in the clubs increases

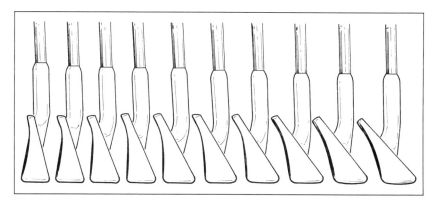

veritable mixture of shots, although the sand wedge is clearly to help you escape from the bunkers. The putter must be chosen wisely, since your relationship with it will inevitably dictate your moods. Your club professional can advise you on every other club in the bag. You must experiment with putters to find the one that most suits you. Remember, it will become either a trusty friend or a fiendish foe. Beware!

HOW TO SELECT YOUR CLUBS

Most of the PGA professionals are very helpful in assisting a beginner to select the equipment that is best for him or her. I could not even begin to suggest which clubs will suit you the most. I can only inform you that such is the range on offer nowadays that there will somewhere be a model which takes your eye. That in itself is one of the tricks, because if a club looks and feels good to you then that is a big step in the right direction. Feeling comfortable with your clubs is, perhaps, more important than anything else.

There is also a range of clubs to suit all pockets. The competition is so intense now that even the less expensive models are extremely well made. Take with a pinch of salt those cries by some manufacturers about using the most expensive clubs in the world. They will not make the millionaire hacker any better,

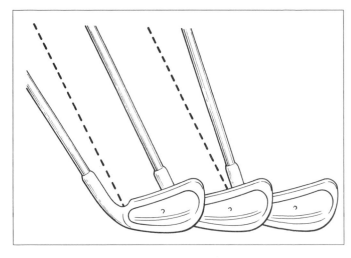

Clubs are now made to suit every potential customer in terms of loft and lie. All clubs pictured here are 5 irons but they show, from left to right, a flat, medium and upright lie

although they might satisfy his ego. But they are not for you. What you must take into account is what feels good for you. Numerous companies now make ranges with clubs that are set up in terms of lofts and lies to suit every potential customer. They offer upright, medium and flat lies. The upright models generally suit the taller player and the flat ones the shorter player. Then you will encounter heel and toe balance, forgiving blades, stiff shafts, flexible shafts etc. Let your club professional guide you through this maze of uncertainty; it is usually a question of trial and error. The local pro will often carry trial sets, so you can experiment.

This is another area where the club pro wins over the high-street shop. In general terms the shops offer a rapid service with the key factor being the profit margin on the clubs they are selling. They buy in bulk, so they want a quick turnover. You might get a better selection, but I doubt whether the service will be as good as that offered by a PGA professional.

For the beginner I believe it is important to find someone who will sell you a set of clubs but at the same time make it clear that if the game doesn't capture your imagination then you can bring the clubs back and get some return on your investment. Which brings us to second-hand clubs. Many professional shops at municipal clubs – those operated by the local authority for the general public – will have a large stock of second-hand clubs. In normal circumstances most professionals at these clubs will allow you to try them out. They have almost certainly been taken in, like a second-hand car, against a new model, so they offer value for money since the shop will already have made a profit on the new set. It is imperative to get set up correctly; to do so, consult your local professional.

GOLF BALLS

Now for the ammunition – golf balls. Over the years the development in this area has been staggering. The golf ball has gone through a scientific metamorphosis from wooden ball to feathery (a leather cover stuffed tight with feathers) to gutty (a solid ball made of a rubbery substance) to today's high-octane, dimpled variety. The dimples are designed to maximise aero-dynamic qualities.

The American size ball (1.68 inches or 42.67 mm) has now been globally accepted so that the British ball (1.62 inches or 41.15 mm) is now being phased out. Both weigh 1.62 ounces or 45.92 grams. The 'big ball', as it has universally become known, is easier to hit. So it is best to start with this one even if it is still possible to purchase some of the smaller variety. The ruling bodies of the game govern the construction of golf balls, so one make of ball does not have any advantage over another in terms of its initial velocity off the club. That, of course, will not stop manufacturers claiming, for instance, that their ball will go further than another model made by a rival company. We are in a competitive market here.

Most professionals prefer to use a wound rubber core ball with a balata cover because it has a high and consistent performance. But, unless you have a bottomless bank account you can forget using balata until you have really mastered the game. It cuts very easily, which is why you will usually see a professional change his ball following a bunker shot because it is so easy to mark. The average amateur, of course, will not worry too much about the odd mark or two, but it is foolish to play with a ball which cuts easily when there are alternatives.

You can buy a low compression one-piece com-position ball which will perform well enough and not cost you the earth. Remember, you are going to lose your fair share of golf balls in the undergrowth. There is also the two-piece construction ball with a durable cover which probably provides a better performance. Manufactur-ers will talk of lively cores, greater distance and better control; they will tell you about the new generation of high-energy core balls which will bring par fives into reach and give you pinpoint accuracy. I have no

There is no doubt that the game is 90 percent skill and 10 percent equipment

doubt that the ball is getting better and better. But as much as good equipment will help to make a player better there is no doubt that the game is really about 90 per cent skill and 10 per cent equipment.

It is probably best to start out with a ball that has a surlyn cover, preferably around a wound centre. You can just about expect the best of both worlds with this type of ball even if it will never give the same spin as a soft balata cover does. Surlyn is a lot harder and more durable, and you can virtually hit it until you lose it. They are expensive – all golf balls are nowadays – but if you can hit it straight (!) then it is possible to get two or three rounds out of one ball.

GOLF BAGS

I think it is a good idea right from the start to buy not only a bag in which to carry all your equipment but also a practice ball bag in which you can put all your rejects. In this way you will gradually build a good supply of balls for taking to the practice range. It might even encourage you to put more work into the game.

As for the bag itself, this is very much a matter of personal choice. I can quite understand that you might want to rush out and buy a big tournament bag (like the one that I have), but I suggest that you don't. Remember that I have a caddie. The only way you are going to move such a huge object around the course is on a trolley, and that will mean additional expense. There are some wonderful carry bags on the market, of all shapes, colours and weights, and the size that you buy will probably depend on the number of clubs you are carrying.

The bag, of course, will house many other things. It will hold your waterproofs – essential garb when it comes to playing the game in Britain – tee pegs, which should be wooden since they do less damage to wooden clubs, gloves, which should fit the hand snugly, pencils for marking the card, markers for spotting the ball on the green, balls and an energy bar or a piece of fruit because you need a snack during the course of a

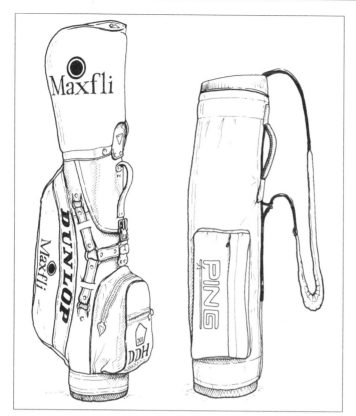

round. I also have a small zip-up bag into which I can put my watch, wedding ring and a handkerchief so that they remain safe and dry. It is also advisable to carry an umbrella, since if a passing shower comes along then you can use that rather than having to step in and out of your waterproofs.

The bag should also have a head cover so that it offers adequate protection for the clubs. There is nothing worse than trying to play the game with wet grips. They slip and slide out of your hands so that you become more and more frustrated. This will become more apparent if you do not look after the grips. Too many amateurs (so this is good advice if you are just starting the game) think only about the time on the course. After a round they throw the clubs into the boot of the car and make for the nineteenth hole. The next time they go out they find the grips are still wet and slippery, rather than slightly tacky which they need to be.

The sensible thing after playing a round in the rain is to take the clubs out of the bag and place them near a radiator or in the drying room which is usually located in the clubhouse locker-room. Then when you get home get a bucket of soapy water and a small scrubbing brush and wash the grips. Wash the soap off and lightly dry them with a towel. After that leave them to dry naturally. Scrubbing the grips with hot, soapy water is the perfect treatment. It makes them tacky again so that they are easier to grip.

The club professional will help you to decide how thick the grips should be to suit your hands. He will probably advise you to use rubber grips since the leather variety require even more care and attention. What you must do is accept that it is your responsibility to keep your equipment in good shape and that if you do not, then only you will be to blame if you fail to make progress.

CLOTHING

Clothing, too, is a matter of personal taste, although you should always feel comfortable in what you wear, and shoes, just like grips, will serve you well as long as you are prepared to look after them. When I was an amateur I was told to look after my hands and my feet. That was after I bought a very cheap pair of hard leather golf shoes. I simply could not break them in. One day I got a terrible blister and the dye in the col-

When buying yourself a pair of golf shoes, buy the best you can afford

ouring of the shoes went into the blister, causing my foot to turn septic. Let that be a lesson to each and every one of you. When it comes to buying yourself a pair of golf shoes, buy the best that you can afford. You will feel the difference. And if you look after them they will last a long, long time. Use shoe trees to dry them out naturally. There is no better treatment than that. Keep them well oiled on the sole and clean on the top. You can buy a pair of rubber shoes for those really wet days, but if you look after your expensive leather ones then they should serve you well.

In the modern era you also have to decide whether to buy shoes with conventional spikes or a pair with rubber soles. The rubber variety are usually lighter and you will notice that, but in my opinion they do not give sufficient support because the sole is flexible. I have also found that they do not grip that well on a dry surface, and they are certainly hopeless on steep slopes in the wet. In fact, you could do yourself an injury. Most certainly, bad shots will result from slipping on the downswing. And the game is difficult enough without making it harder.

4 WHAT TO DO IN THE MEANTIME

In my opinion no one golfer has an absolutely pure swing. So from the standpoint of providing you with tips it is important to get one thing right from the start. It is imperative that you sift through all the information you assemble, be it from this book, other books, magazines, television, your club professional or by watching tournament golf, and use the bits which you fully understand. For instance, my feeling is that the instructional articles in golf magazines have become increasingly good, but conversely they can

Treat every book on the game, every magazine, every article, every tip with a great deal of caution

also complicate things and confuse people. Therefore my immediate advice is to treat every book on the game, every magazine, every article, every tip with a great deal of caution, because you cannot take anything as gospel in this game. One tip might work for one person on one day and not on another, and it might never work for you at all.

How can it be any other way? Things with golf 'ain't what they ought to be' according to the mechanics of the game. For it is indisputable that golf is a game of contradictions. For a start, if you hit down on a ball then it goes up. If you attempt to hit the ball up then it will inevitably bumble along the ground. If you hit through the ball severely to the right then it is on the cards that you will hook it to the left. Then, if you come across the ball, taking the club from out to in, you will slice the ball to the right. And if you come

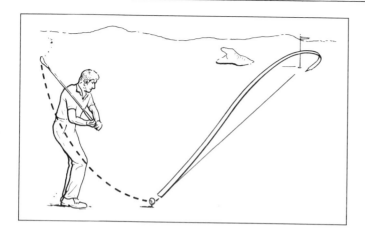

The ball paths of a hook ...
and a slice

to think about it, for the majority of us who play the game right-handed it is the left side which dominates the shot!

That is the theory, to which my answer is 'to thine own self be true'. In other words, since no swing can be exactly the same as another, you will decide what is best for you. You will discover over the years what does and doesn't work for you. The basic premise to remember is that very few exponents of the game, amateur or professional, ever change their swing.

What I hope to do in this chapter is not to preach to you about the golf swing but to offer a few tips, gathered over the years by me and others, which I believe will help you to become a better golfer.

First and foremost I cannot emphasise enough how important it is to give yourself time to prepare for a round of golf. Now I know this is easier said than done. For many of you it is a case of squeezing in nine holes after school before the homework has to be done. And I know it is difficult for the shop owner **Give yourself time to prepare** with early closing on a Wednesday to **thoroughly for a round of golf** do anything but drive to the course, take out his clubs and rush to the first tee.

Yet there is no surer way of failing to get complete satisfaction from a round of golf. In your panic to get to the tee you have momentarily lost all sense of rhythm. And the golf swing is all about tempo. So you heave into that first shot and, surprise, surprise, the ball soars away at a right angle towards out of bounds. You leave the first green with a seven on the card, completely dispirited. However, I am equally fully aware that the Wednesday afternoon dash is all a bit of a swindle. You really *do* have a little time on your hands, except that it is reserved for a couple of pints and a sausage sandwich with the gathering lads before you split into threes and fours. Battle commences with a burp rather than a birdie.

I am not about to interfere with that. Golf has enriched many people's lives because of the pleasure derived from the nineteenth hole; and long may that be the case. But what I must stress is that if you do have designs on becoming, say, a single-handicap golfer, then getting to the course on time will help you to consummate a winning relationship with the game.

TEN TIPS

Below are ten tips concerning all aspects of the game which I hope will help you to become a better golfer.

1. Arrive at the course in good time. Part of the professional routine includes mental preparation. For that reason it is imperative to get ready in a manner which suits your game and your personality. Most

professionals will get to the course at least two hours before they tee off. I would suggest that for, the average amateur thirty minutes is sufficient. Think of it in this way. If you are going to be on the course for three to four hours (I hope the former because slow play is becoming a thorn in the side of golf) then it is worthwhile hitting a few shots to ensure that you arrive on the first tee mentally and physically relaxed. Quite honestly it does not matter if you don't always hit the ball well on the practice range. Some of my very best rounds have followed poor pre-round sessions. The reason for that is that I always stand on the first tee knowing that I have given myself more than adequate time to prepare. Always spend the last few minutes on the practice putting green.

2. It helps to dress well. You don't have to be a flash Harry. You don't have to wear plus-twos – although they are not a bad idea in wet weather if you spend a lot of time in the rough! – or monogrammed socks like the Australian Rodger Davis. What is important is to dress so that you feel good. In other words, keep your

Always try to be well dressed on the course

shoes, as well as your clubs, clean so that when you look down as you take your stance everything looks pristine. You'll be surprised how much that helps you mentally.

3. Know the rules – it is surprising how many shots it could save you. One endearing aspect of golf is that we basically police ourselves. If we do cheat then we cheat only ourselves. I find it difficult to reprimand those who do – they have only my sympathy. If they can't play the game fair and square then that is up to them; very soon they will find themselves short of partners. Apart from that there is little doubt that a lot of newcomers to the game – and old hands come to that – unknowingly break the rules. Moreover, they do not know the rules well enough to employ them to their advantage. For the 'Rules of Golf' – and there are many of them – have been written to make the game as fair as possible. So it makes sense that on occasions you will hit the ball into a position from which you are entitled to take relief without being penalised. You will have a greater understanding of the rules if you make the time to read them and remember to carry a book of them with you at all times. The governing body of the game in Great Britain is the Royal and Ancient Golf Club of St Andrews, while across the Atlantic it is the United States Golf Association based in New Jersey. If you have trouble obtaining a copy of the rules then you should contact the Golf Foundation from whom they are available free of charge.

4. If conditions make it impossible to play, and you have a little time on your side, then check out your alignment in a mirror. Without wishing to delve too deeply into the mechanics of the game I would say that the first fundamental of golf is to appreciate the importance of a good grip and to accept that the best golfers play the ball from a similar position every time – between the left heel and the centre of the stance. This you should have learned from your club professional, but it is very easy to get out of alignment. So use a mirror to ensure that you are setting up right. You

Opposite:
Setting-up, using
golf clubs as a
guide

will also discover that it is possible to check through the swing by using the mirror. You will learn to detect faults in your own game. But beware of one thing: it is very easy to correct one fault with another, and that will only make the game more difficult. Leave that to your local club professional – it's **Bear in mind that it is very easy to** definitely worth using some of the **correct one fault with another** paper-round money for a thirty-minute lesson.

5. If you are fortunate enough to have the room, why not purchase a practice net for the garden? The real tip here is only to obtain one that is large enough and secure enough. It is no good if the ball flies out of the neck of the club and goes through the neighbour's window! And, remember, you are going to have to stand three or four yards back from the net so it must half-envelop you for safety reasons. My friend Mark James has a reinforced net which he uses throughout the winter months when at home. His launching pad, so to speak, is a large piece of astro-turf, so he can use it even when it has snowed. The obvious alternative is to use the practice facilities at your club or to find a nearby driving range. I can also recommend air balls. They are rather like foam rubber with a pellet in the middle. You can give them a good hit and I assure you it does feel like a real golf ball. So they are a particularly good practice aid because you can take a full swing without needing a net. They travel about 30 yards at most, so you can use them virtually anywhere. They help to train your eyes to keep looking at the ball and improve your timing. Air balls are cheap to buy, and your local professional probably stocks them.

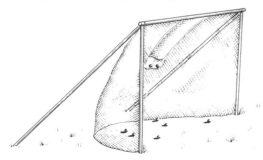

If you have room, buy a practice net for the garden

Opposite: The correct alignment when using an iron

A complete,
controlled, swing
sequence

10

6. I have lost count of the number of times that I have stood on the practice range and seen youngsters arrive only immediately to remove the driver from the bag. Most professionals will start a practice session by hitting a few little wedge shots; it helps to loosen the muscles. What is more, if we learn to chip well then we can save shots each round. I don't have a big garden, and it is ideal for only about a 20-yard chip shot, but I have worked out a practice routine which helps me and I'm sure would improve your game. What I do is chip to a specific target with the idea of landing the ball on the mark every time. I do not worry where the ball eventually finishes. In other words, you can get the feel for landing the ball on a 10-yard marker, or one at 15 yards, or even 20 yards and more if you have the room. This teaches you control of the swing, because these shots are all about 'feel'. You will learn in time how the ball runs out to the hole. So when you face a recovery shot from around the green, the first objective is to pick out the spot where you must land the ball so that it finishes closes to the hole. By practising in the garden you will have edged towards mastering the art of pitching the ball on to a certain spot. And remember not always to give yourself a good lie. When you miss a green, do you always get a good lie? Think about it.

> Most professionals will start a practice session by hitting a few little wedge shots to loosen up

7. If the weather really is awful then there is no alternative but to practise indoors. If you have the right kind of carpet, one on which you can get a good roll on the ball, then at least you will have an opportunity to groove your putting stroke. This can be done in several different ways. You can putt to a specific target. You can putt to an exact distance. You can use table or chair legs, although in time there will be a certain amount of wear and tear! So I think it is best to use a cup or a glass as a target. You can also buy special putting aids which return the ball to you – if you hole it!

8. A good tip for keeping the swing in good shape

during the winter, on those cold or very wet days when it is impossible to play because the greens are frozen or waterlogged, is to use a broom or a brush. If you just swing slowly, getting a good rhythm going, then it will help to promote a slower, flowing action rather than a very quick, wristy one. The swing has got to be controlled, and this exercise will also give you a little bit of extra pull because of the weight of the brush head. I believe this to be an excellent way of obtaining the right speed for your swing. You can also work on that little pause at the top of the swing which can make all the difference.

9. I do not think that the late Henry Cotton, with whom I worked in the early 1970s, will mind me passing on his tyre routine. The idea is to take an old car tyre, without the wheel, and then gently tap it with an old club. You can use first both hands, then your left hand on its own and then the right. The aim is to educate the hands to play the game properly.

10. There is a plethora of books on the game, so we should have no trouble in finding some bed-time reading. Some books, of course, are written from an entertainment standpoint. Others detail instruction and are mostly written by well-known golfers in collaboration with recognised authors. It is not my intention to recommend specific books to you. There are many fine ones about and you must pay your money and make your choice. What I would say is that when you are reading one and something actually makes a lot of sense with regard to your own swing, then immediately jot that down in a notebook. Later, try it out. It might be something minor such as gripping the club a little tighter with the right hand. But what you must do is monitor the progress, if any, that you achieve by making that change. We all know the fundamentals of the golf game – weight on the instep, moving on to the back foot and then through again. Sometimes you just need something to set off the movement. It is in these kinds of areas that books and magazines, with instructional detail, can assist.

5 FITNESS AND DIET

Let us get one thing straight from the start: I do not want to preach to you about fitness or diet. You should know what is best for your body. I think that most of us ignore at some time every day what the doctors and dieticians say is best for us. That is the way of the world. If we conformed all the time, or if we believed everything we were told, then I am sure it would become a fairly dull world.

It is, of course, important to feel healthy. At the same time it is true that the average amateur golfer need not be as finely tuned an athlete as the professional. It should be obvious to anybody with an interest in the game that at the top level there is intense mental as well as physical strength. So an alert and sound mind is as important as rippling muscles.

Golf is not a question of becoming Charles Atlas. Indeed, 'Popeye-arms' can remove the feel that a golf-

Golf is certainly not a question of becoming Charles Atlas
er needs, just like a jockey whose hands and arms become an extension of the reins. In golf, so much of the time it is how you *feel* a shot that counts. The newcomer to the game will not entirely understand this. Basically you will discover as you progress the significance of learning to feel the shot. It will not come easily, because the muscles we use for golf do not work in harmony.

Opposite:
Seve Ballesteros
keeps fit for golf
Indeed, when you first start playing you will almost certainly use muscles that are not needed and so this

will make it difficult for you to co-ordinate your body actions. Then hitting a shot becomes hard work and you will begin to be discouraged. This is why we need mental discipline so that we can accumulate a wealth of knowledge and assemble it so that it makes the game easier.

You will learn, too, the advantage of having strong legs. If we are to stand firm to the ball then the stronger we are in the thigh area, the hitting area, the better. The grip must be firm but not too tight, so it is also important that we exercise our wrists. To emphasize the importance of strong legs I can tell you that one of the most vital pieces of equipment that Severiano Ballesteros has at home is a bicycle. Most of us have jogged over the years at one time or another to improve our overall stamina and build up our legs. Some doctors will advise us not to jog because we can place pressure on the back. But I know of no reason why cycling should be discouraged. Seve, of course, lives in northern Spain and he has made good use of the mountainous terrain near his home in Pedrena. He is encouraged, too, by the fact that he thoroughly enjoys cycling. Only hours after winning the Open at Royal Lytham in 1988 he was glued to the television watching the progress of Pedro Delgado in the Tour de France. (Delgado won!)

The teacher David Leadbetter has concentrated on improving Nick Faldo's stance. With Nick being 6 feet 3 inches tall it is inevitable that he is not as evenly balanced as, say, Tom Watson. Nick, too, enjoys cycling so that is a help, but he really has to work at being firm at the address position in the swing. Sandy Lyle is also very tall, but he is built differently to Nick. His legs are shorter and so he has less trouble in this area. Even so, he works hard on physical fitness. He runs quite a bit and he uses the conventional exercise bicycle and rowing machine. I make a point of naming players like Seve, Nick and Sandy as a way to impress upon you that golf is not simply a matter of walking out on to the course for four hours and hitting a little white ball from A to B.

Opposite:
Nick Faldo who has
one of the most
stylish swings

If you want to become proficient at the subject then, like anything else, you must be prepared to devote an enormous amount of time and attention to it.

WARMING UP

If you are playing in a medal round, or a competition, and you want to get the best results from your game, then first and foremost you must be ready to warm up. I have already stressed the importance of giving yourself ample time to prepare for a round of golf. I believe that, if time is on our side, then we must start to prepare even before we get to the course.

I would reiterate that my suggestions might not either fit your lifestyle or be as beneficial to you as they are to me. Even so, I think that a bath or shower to loosen the muscles is always a good idea before venturing forth to the first tee. However, a lot of people prefer not to have one, being of the opinion that it might leave you too relaxed. I understand that viewpoint, but I believe that most of us suffer in one way or another with our backs so it is vital that we do all we can to loosen it before we move into action. Therefore a shower or bath is essential as far as I am concerned, since I am a sufferer.

The golf swing is alien to the body, so it is difficult to protect the back. If you think about it, even practice putting puts a strain on the back; it means that for some time you are stooping over. That is unnatural, so we must do all that we can to ensure that we are assisting the back to absorb the pressure under which we will place it in the pursuit of golfing perfection. Contra-exercises are a first-rate way to help the back along. It stands to reason that if we are forever bending forward then we should do exercises bending backwards.

In warm weather you will obviously not need to be so concerned about loosening the muscles as you are when there is a nip in the air. But it is still important to train the eye for the day. This will entail hitting a few balls, even if they are air balls. In this situation you are not practising for the sake of it.

Opposite:
Sandy Lyle runs and
uses an exercise
bicycle to keep fit

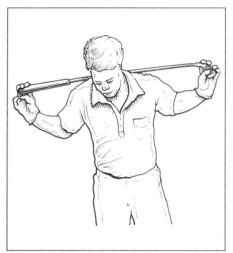
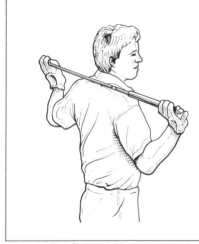

A useful exercise for loosening the back muscles

You are attempting to feel the swing for the day and to find the target. I am not talking about the middle of the fairway or the green. The target in this instance is the ball. We must train our eyes to focus on it and our hands to find it. I remember when I went down to Portugal to practise with Henry Cotton, he would walk between shots with a club in his hand. He was forever swinging it with one hand, not in a full arc but simply, for instance, to clip the tops of daisies on the fairways. He was teaching his hands to find the target. What is more, by holding the club in one hand and swinging it he was also exercising his wrists.

In fact, you can use a club to do a number of exercises which should be beneficial to your game. For instance, put the club horizontally behind your back and lock it in your arms, then simply turn from side to side. This will send a message to the muscles that need to work during the golf swing. So it is not a bad idea to do a few on the first tee. For if the muscles are lazy then it is conceivable that you will make a slow start. And that first hole is more important than I can stress. This is a first-class example of how, if we are physically right to tee off so that we start the round with a par, it can only help to improve our mental outlook for the round.

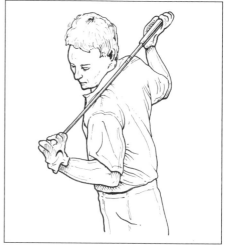

I respect that amateurs will be involved in a lot of match-play golf, so that if you have have a poor first hole you are only one down, or will play to the Stableford format – a point system devised by Dr Frank Stableford, a member of the Royal Liverpool and Wallasey Clubs, in 1931 – so that you lose nothing since points are gained for eagles, birdies, pars and bogies but not for double bogies or anything upwards. So it is only in medal play – a contest where all strokes are accumulated – that, say, an eight or a nine at the first will really hurt. But the power of positive thinking is as important in golf as it is in any other walk of life and we will surely be thinking more positively if we move to the second tee one up on our opponent or with three Stableford points on our scorecard.

The Stableford format, an alternative to the match-play format

So if you feel a little stiffer than usual when you get on the first tee, why not warm up with two clubs in your hands by swinging them very gently to and fro. It will untie any knots that are there, although later, with only one club in your hands, be careful not to swing too quickly at the ball. Think tempo all the time, and then these exercises will be more beneficial to you.

Let me also emphasize that I do not participate in too many strenuous exercises because I do not want to become ultra-tight. You do not need to be muscle-bound to play golf. In fact, it is a hindrance rather than a help. If you are particularly weak then, fair enough, you could start a weight-training programme, although I cannot stress enough the importance of good supervision in this area. If you can afford it then it might be a good idea to join one of the health clubs that are springing up all over the country. Most of them also have pools, and swimming is a relaxing way to keep in good shape. Pumping too much iron can develop muscles that might be disadvantageous to the swing. So you must search for the right balance, and I have a high regard for swimming because it keeps the upper body well toned while at the same time strengthening the legs.

DIET

Diet, as we are repeatedly and reliably informed nowadays, is as important as exercise. I had a lot of back trouble about four years ago and since then I have taken more care with my diet. I delved into the subject to ascertain whether there were foods that were good or bad for me. In fact it was my chiropractor who pointed out that it would be wholesome for me to cut out red meats. On the basis of that I made a considerable effort to reduce my intake of them. I do not expect anybody to become a vegetarian overnight, although nowadays I personally rarely eat red meats – beef, lamb, pork or fattier meats. I eat chicken and fish, pasta and plenty of fruit. I still eat chips, but my diet includes lots of vegetables.

I have come round to a diet which starts with a **It is extremely difficult to produce** healthy breakfast with plenty of rough-**your best on a full stomach** age. I never eat a large lunch, because I am either playing or practising in the afternoons. It is extremely difficult to produce your best on a full stomach; you feel tired, and the doctors stress that the body is using its energies to digest the food so that you will be less well equipped to fight off the bogies!

A lot of people have spoken to me about the value of sugar in the diet. As far as I am concerned, as a layman of the subject, it is a tricky problem that I would be best not to approach in a book such as this. I do not rate particularly highly the value of sugar, although I am sure you would get a more in-depth answer from a dietician. I myself do not take sugar in tea or coffee; I suppose I basically feel that sugar puts weight on. I certainly do not advise the drinking of sugar-filled fizzy drinks – they give you a bloated feeling, and one thing that you cannot do if you feel that way is to play good golf.

You can help yourself on the course by carrying good old-fashioned water. I always carry some fruit. You will often see a golfer munching on a banana, because they are extremely nutritious. Chocolate, too, can provide you with additional energy, as can the modern-day energy bars; these energy bars apparently give you a slow release of energy rather than the quick release that comes from sugar-based items.

Quite frankly, it is all a matter of personal choice. You must decide what is best for you, because it is your body. We can share opinions on smoking and drinking but we can only decide ourselves at the end of the day whether or not we *wish* to partake. I certainly steer clear of alcohol when I am playing golf. I might enjoy the odd glass or two of wine with my dinner and, maybe, a beer or two at the very end of a tournament. The rules of my profession instruct us firmly against drinking on the course, although I would never consider doing so anyway. Even when the round ends I would advise that you do not head straight for the nineteenth hole, even if your tipple is orange juice. It is a good idea to wind down, let the muscles relax and consider some of the shots you have played. Again, I think it advisable to have a shower after a round, because it refreshes you and returns the body to the right temperature.

Remember, too, that in order to keep yourself fit and well it is always best to wear good clothing to combat the wet and wild conditions that we so often experience on British golf courses. Therefore, make sure that you purchase a set of waterproofs

that provide more than adequate protection against the wind and rain. I suggest a roll-neck sweater in very cold weather and a slipover at most times, because it does afford the back even greater support. You will often see Lee Trevino wearing one in warm weather and that could well be because his back is playing up.

Back at home there is no reason not to take exercise, even if you do not possess a bicycle or a rowing machine. I use a golf club by holding the grip with my arms out straight from my body and then waggling the club by some eight inches side to side, or east to west, then north to south and then in a circle, clockwise then anti-clockwise. I repeat the exercise probably twenty times. After that, take two minutes' rest and repeat the exercise. If you can manage a few more then by all means go ahead. You will find that it strengthens the forearms and the wrists.

To keep the wrists strong is very important. I must emphasize that we have to train ourselves to allow the shock of hitting the ball to pass through the shaft of the club rather than into our hands, which would weaken our grip. A common fault in amateur swings is loosening the left-

(Opposite): Make sure you dress appropriately for the weather conditions

To keep the wrists strong at impact is very important

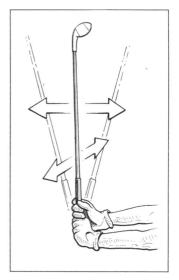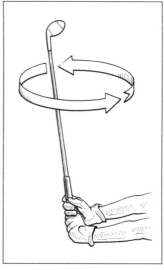

Strong wrists are very important

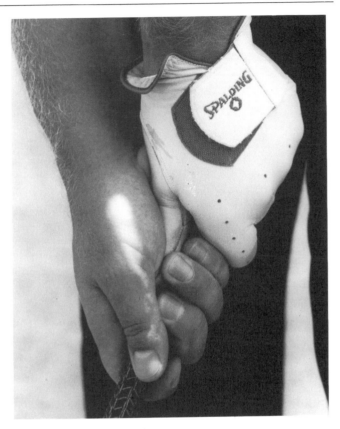

A common fault with amateurs is the loosening of the left hand

hand grip. Immediately this happens you are locked into hitting from the top of the swing, and with the body rather than the hands, so anything can happen. It is therefore worthwhile to work on keeping our wrists strong.

With this in mind we can build a makeshift weight device which includes a length of strong string some five feet long, a small wooden handle to which to tie the string and a weight at the other end of the string. It can be any kind of weight and it need not be too heavy because the exercise is extremely strenuous. You should hold on to the wood, stretch out your arms and wind in the string, with the weight attached. This is why the string should not be more than five feet long, as we do not want it to touch the ground. Once you have wound the weight to the top then you

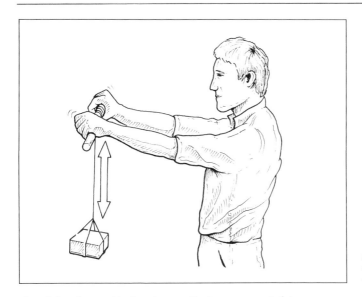

A wrist-strengthening exercise

should release it slowly so that you are taking every bit of the force from the weight. This can be done as many times as you like.

For many of you a round of golf will take up as much time as you can spare. But if you can make the time here and there to try some of these suggestions then I am confident that they will help you not only to be healthier but also to play better golf. Even carrying a tennis ball with you everywhere you go can help. Squeeze it in the left hand and then in the right. This will strengthen the hands and wrists. It can be as easy as that.

6 LEARNING FROM OTHERS

Television is basically a medium to entertain; yet it can also educate, and golf is a fine example of this process. For it is a fact that a lot of professionals watch other professionals at tournaments because they gain feedback which might benefit their own game. Some golfers, for instance, will take time out to pull up a chair and sit for maybe an hour watching another player hit balls on the practice range. Seve, of course, becomes one of the stars of that particular show.

As it is unlikely that you have the chance to attend tournaments regularly, then most of your watching is probably done from an armchair. This is where you can sit back and be entertained – and educated! You can learn from the rhythm of the swing. You can learn the art of course management. You can learn simply by watching that the bunker shot, feared by so many amateurs, is not that difficult to execute. And you can piece all this knowledge together to take shots off your handicap.

Over the years I have learnt most about the golf swing by watching other players I honestly believe that over the years I have learnt most about the golf swing by watching other players. In recent months I have been fortunate enough to have David Leadbetter, the teacher who remodelled Nick Faldo's swing prior to him winning the Open Championship at Muirfield, refining my own swing. That means to say that I am lucky enough to have 'inside knowledge'. So when it

Opposite:
Seve Ballesteros,
an inspiration to
all golfers

comes to the average amateur looking to improve his game, there can be little doubt that watching other players is the smart thing to do.

For a start, it can whet your appetite to play the game. How many of us as kids watched the Cup Final then raced along to the local common for a kick-about? Well, it is now the same with golf. Who would not want to be on the links minutes after seeing Seve hitting that adroit chip inches from the hole at the last to win the Open Championship at Royal Lytham and St Annes for a third time?

The importance of wanting to play cannot be over-emphasized. It comes to all of us – that stale feeling when you lack the reserve required to produce your best. I often video tournaments and I can tell you that, apart from gaining a tip or two as I watch, they often send me back to the fairways, or the practice range, filled with renewed enthusiasm for the game. You see, to play golf you cannot go out and force shots. If you are enjoying yourself then all manner of different types of shots will seem that much easier to you.

Seve unquestionably inspires me, and I am sure he does you. He simply stands up to the ball, oozing with confidence, and makes a full, solid swing every time. He doesn't hold back. I don't mean that he thrashes the ball. He has, more than anybody else in the modern game, turned the swing into an art form. He makes it look easy, with that wonderful rhythm; and he has such a 'feel' for the game that he can execute the most marvellous shots.

When we watch golf, especially on TV, it is, of course, not always Seve who is on the screen. You might even get a glimpse of Howard Clark now and then! But seriously, you may wonder on occasions how certain players with strange actions ever get the ball into the air, let alone win tournaments. Basically it is because the individual has created his own method which works for him. It might not look a text-book swing but I can assure you the expert eye will soon tune in to all the good things about it.

Opposite:
Watching others
play

Lee Trevino, of course, has that open stance, but he has two Open Championships, two US Opens and two US PGA Championships to prove that it has not hindered him. You have probably watched Eamonn Darcy and come to wonder why he has won so many titles. Well, the one thing that all good players possess is the ability to square the club head up to the line of flight during contact with the ball. Let me assure you that Eamonn does exactly that. And he hits through the ball; he does not hold back. He has a full, flowing swing. There might not be beauty in Eamonn's swing, but there is rhythm. The importance of rhythm is to ensure a smooth take-away, a brief pause at the top and a downswing that isn't rushed. Eamonn is no different from any other player in that when he loses his rhythm he loses the ability to hit the ball accurately. It is clear evidence that this game depends so much on tempo.

All good players possess the ability to square the club head up to the line of the flight during contact with the ball

Miller Barber, now playing on the US Seniors Tour, has a mean-looking swing. In my opinion it is awful. But he has the ability to get the ball from A to B, and he possesses a natural talent for returning the club head back from all types of angles to be square upon impact with the ball. Then take the case of Calvin Peete. He suffered a broken left elbow as a child and even today he cannot extend the arm. So much for the theory which so many experts expound on having a straight left arm. Calvin's is bent, and I know that from 1981 through to 1987 he headed the American Tour's statistical charts for driving accuracy.

So that in itself is a tip when you are watching TV: there is something good to be extracted from every swing. Let us face the fact that there have been many fantastic swings which have not achieved as much as some funny-looking ones. David Leadbetter, for instance, says that he dismantled a Nick Faldo swing that was aesthetically pleasing but which in his opinion would never stand up to the pressure of winning a major championship. Nick may have won a major with his old swing; we shall never know. But

Opposite:
Nick Faldo re-modelled his swing and won the Open

he *did* win the Open with the Leadbetter swing.

What Nick had already mastered, and what I and other professionals would like to believe that we possess, is the art of course management. This is where television can really assist you if you devote time and attention to watching the players. When we are young – and it is perfectly natural – we all want to hit the ball the proverbial country mile. We want to get that big stick out and give the ball one heck of a crack. So it is as well to watch and see just how many times a professional reverts to an iron for safety. Of course, not too many people can hit a one iron like Sandy Lyle – and I include professionals! But if you learn from the professionals then you will be able to see that at the club where you play it might be better to use, say, a four wood off the tee at a particular hole rather than a driver.

Most certainly watching television will help you to rationalise specific shots. I spoke at the start of this chapter about bunker shots being easier to play than most people believe. They are – they really are. The reasoning behind that will become more apparent if you watch the stars on TV. You will rarely see **You will rarely see a professional make** a professional make a snatchy swing in **a snatchy swing in a bunker** a bunker. It is in normal circumstances a three-quarter swing built into a very flow ing action. Most amateurs rush into the shot. That is absolutely fatal. I'm not saying that you will always get the ball close to the hole if you follow the professional way, but I do believe you will on most occasions get the ball out of the sand.

To help put your mind at rest in this area, just watch how the professionals usually get the ball closer to the hole from out of a bunker than they do from a difficult lie in the rough around the green. I can assure you that it is easier to play a shot from out of a bunker which is well kept than many other recovery shots. You see, from a bunker you can dictate the way that **Opposite:** you want the ball to drop on to the green. You can **The bunker shot** land the ball soft or hard. You can play it with less **is one of the** spin so that the ball runs further. You can see all of **easiest in golf**

this and more on television.

ROUTINE

Television, too, can help you to build a routine. This is an important facet of the game which is too often overlooked. In this area you can look for a player who has a routine which you believe it is possible to copy. It does not have to be a Seve Ballesteros or a Greg Norman – although both have outstanding routines. One of the best routines as far as I am concerned is that of Gary Player. He sets up and visualises the shot he must make, checks his yardage, checks his stance, usually absolutely square to the target, takes one last, hard look at the ball and then kicks the right knee in before starting the backswing. Watch for that kick. To Gary it is very important. It is what we call the trigger.

Every player, however good or bad he or she might be, needs their own release button to take the club back. I recall that only days before Seve won the Open at Royal Lytham in 1988 he revealed that the problems he was having with his swing stemmed from not being able to take the club back. It happens to everybody. I would recommend just gripping a little tighter with the right index finger or pressing the thumb down on the top of the club. Anything like that will provide the trigger for a swing which takes little more than two seconds to complete.

So keep watching the television screen, and going to tournaments if you can, to study a player with a routine which you think will suit you. Then, of course, you can adapt parts of it. Think in terms of the way you take the club out of the bag. The way you look at the ball and the target line. Then put the club face to the target line along which you will be attempting to hit, and then take your stance. It should never be the other way around. You must imagine that the club head is going to be hitting square to the ball all the time.

A sound routine is a vital ingredient of the golf swing

I believe that the more that you watch the leading players in action the more you will come to realise

Opposite:
Gary Player, a superb example of the dedicated professional

that a sound routine is a vital ingredient of the swing. Routine, too, is of paramount importance when it comes down to that game within a game – putting. There is unquestionably no doubt that putting is the most individualistic part of golf. I honestly cannot think of more than two or three players with putting styles that resemble each other. They all, of course, follow the basic code which is to take the putter back smoothly and return it naturally through the ball. It is how they set up, feel and see each putt which should be of interest to you.

Putting is an exact science, but a lot of people will look at a putt and see everything breaking left to right, possibly because one eye is stronger than the other. This you will not be able to determine by watching. But you will see that the trick of the stroke is to start the putter square to the line along which you want to hit and then move the club head back so that it opens ever so slightly. Quite frankly, it doesn't matter how you stand to the ball. That you will definitely spot, because so many different stances are adopted.

Now look to find another routine which you feel that you can integrate into your game. A routine enables you to keep thinking and relieves the tension and the pressure. You could, for instance, think in terms of having two practice putting strokes behind or to the side of the ball. Then get the putter behind the ball and settle into a comfortable position. Look two or three times along the target line towards the hole, count to two and make the stroke.

You will not make every putt. But then it is as well to remember that the game allows for you to take 36 putts each round – two at each hole. That is why it is generally accepted that putting makes all the difference between winning and losing. Once you have grooved your game then it is fair to assume that you will play fairly consistently from tee to green. The intangible aspect is whether or not you will putt well. Some days you stroke the ball with grace and precision and for some reason it lips the edge of the hole time and time again. You will see this with watching

Opposite:
Sandy Lyle, virtually unbeatable when he is putting well

the professionals. You will understand their frustration when it happens to you.

Even so, I do believe that as an amateur, and this most certainly applies to those with handicaps in double figures, a good putting round is not the way to reduce your handicap. The way to do that is in being able to weigh up every shot that you must make with a calm inner strength that exudes confidence. And that confidence comes not so much from believing, because you have seen Seve fire an astonishing recovery shot through a narrow gap from out of the trees, that you, too, can make it. No, it stems from realising that you have more chance of salvaging if you make your first priority getting back to the fairway and your next reaching the green.

I have seen more amateurs than I care to mention come to grief because they have got themselves into a situation where they start wondering how Seve would manufacture some kind of miracle shot. There is no real benefit in watching golf if you are going to take that kind of thought with you to the fairways. You must never forget that Seve, and all professionals, are not only experts of their trade but also entertainers. So by all means allow yourself to be entertained by such strokes of genius, but thereafter always consider what is the best way for you to save shots.

All professionals decide how risky a shot is before they play it. You must do the same, but from the standpoint that it requires years of discipline to execute certain shots. I do not mean to wag a disciplinary finger at you. Sure, there are times when it is hard to resist trying to find that gap out of the forest. Or letting rip into a three **The harder you practise the luckier you'll get, as Gary Player said** wood to see if you can't get up at a par five in two. You've just had a hard day, so why shouldn't you squeeze every ounce of enjoyment you can from this great game?

Go ahead, and do so with my blessing. If, however, you should become a very serious player, then to paraphrase Gary Player always remember the harder you practise the luckier you'll get.

Opposite:
Learning to read
putts is an art

7 GLOSSARY

Aboard On the green

Ace A hole made in one stroke; most commonly achieved at a par three hole

Address Stance adopted by a player before hitting the ball

Air-mailed Said of a ball that goes over the green without touching the putting surface

Albatross Known also as a Double Eagle; the term for a score of three under par at one hole

Approach The shot to the green

Apron The grass area immediately bordering the putting green; it is generally mowed lower than the green

Arc The path of the hands, arms and club from the commencement to the completion of the swing

Away A golfer is away when it is his turn to play

Backdoor A putt which hits the back of the cup before dropping into the hole from the far side

Backswing Movement of hands, arms and club away from the ball

Baff To strike the ball with the sole of the club head and so send the ball into the air

Baffy The term for a hickory-shafted club, similar to the modern four wood, employed for hitting lofted shots

Banana shot A very badly spliced shot sending the ball violently from left to right through the air

Baseball grip A two-handed grip in which the fingers of the two hands neither overlap nor interlock

Better-ball Two players on the same side, each playing their own ball with the lower score of the two counting at each hole

Birdie The term applied for a score of one under par at one hole

Bisque A handicap stroke taken at a hole already played at the recipient's choice

Blind hole One where the green cannot be seen by the player when the approach shot is being executed

Bogey In strict terms the number of strokes which an average player should take at a hole. In America this term refers to a score of one

Borrow
over par at one specific hole and in Britain it is nowadays used with the same meaning
Slope or undulation of a green

Bowling alley
A slang expression for an extremely narrow fairway

Brassie
An original term for a wooden club, with a brass sole plate, which today is known as a two wood

Break
A reference to the percentage of turn which there might be in a specific putt

Bulger
An original term for a wooden club with a convex face

Bunker
Hazards which originated from sheep burrowing for shelter in the sand dunes; they are also known as sand traps

Bye
The holes which remain after a match between players has been concluded; a modest side-stake is often entered into at this stage if a money match has been played

Can
A slang term for holing a putt which is also sometimes used to refer to the hole itself

Carry
The distance from where the ball is struck to where it lands

Casual water
Snow, ice and any temporary accumulation of water, not usually to be found on the course, from where a player can pick up and drop his ball without incurring a penalty

Chip
A shot to the flag made from close to the green which is usually out of the rough encircling the green

Chip and run
A shot purposely hit low so that it lands on the green then rolls towards the flag

Cleek
A hickory-shafted club which is equal to the two iron of today; it had an iron head and was used for driving and sometimes for putting

Cock
The bending of the wrists on the backswing. The wrists are uncocked on the downswing

Concede
The act of a player accepting that his opponent has won the ball; it mostly applies to a putt being conceded as a ball has finished so close to the hole

Cross bunker
A reference to a bunker that is in a fairway area so that it requires a player to hit over it on the way from the tee to the green

Course rating
The evaluation of the difficulty of a course based on its overall yardage

Croquet putting
Putting, as in croquet, by swinging the club between the legs; it was ruled illegal in 1967

Cup
Generally recognised as an American expression, or slang, for the hole in which the flag stands

Cuppy
A small depression in which the ball may lie

Cut
The term for a ball which moves left to right, although missing the cut applies to when a player fails to qualify for the remaining 36 holes of a 72-hole tournament

Dead
A ball is said to be dead when it lies so near the hole that the putt is an absolute certainty

Divot
Slice of turf displaced in

the execution of a stroke and which should be replaced immediately by the player

Dormie A player is said to be 'dormie' when he is ahead by the number of holes which remain in a match

Double eagle American colloquialism for an albatross, i.e. three under par at one particular hole

Draw To make the ball move slightly from right to left through the air

Drive The shot with the driver

Driver The club usually employed for striking the first shot at par four or par five holes. The head is larger than the head of any other club in the bag and the angle of loft is usually less than 12 degrees

Duck hook A shot which unintentionally bends sharply from right to left

Eagle The term applied for a score of two under the specified par at one hole

Eclectic Competition played over a given number of rounds, the player counting his best score at each hole

Equity Decision not covered by the rules

Face Area of the club head which strikes the ball

Fade A stroke which through the air moves the ball from left to right

Fairway That part of a hole which is usually mown short so that it forms a 'channel' from the tee to the green

Feathery Ball made of feathers encased in leather; in common use until the mid-nineteenth century

Feel A sense of touch, particularly over the shorter shots around the green

Flat Swing in which the arc is closer to a horizontal than a vertical plane

Flight Trajectory of the ball

Fluff As with the duff, hitting ground behind the ball

Fog Moss or rank grass

Fore Warning shout to other players in danger of being hit by a ball in flight

Foozle A bad, bungling stroke

Forecaddie A 'ball spotter' sometimes used in areas of the course where a ball can be lost

Forward press Forward movement of the body to release tension before beginning the backswing

Fourball Four players in teams of two, each playing their own ball

Foursome A match in which two golfers play on each side. Each pair of players share a ball, hitting alternate shots at any given hole and alternating hole by hole when teeing off

Freeze Inability to begin the backswing, brought about by nerves. Most common when putting

Fried egg A slang expression for a ball buried in a bunker

Fringe See *Apron*

Get up and down To pitch or chip then one putt

Gobble An original term for a well-struck hard putt which, had it not gone into the hole, would have gone some distance beyond

Grain The way that the grass lies on a green, as with cats' fur

Grand slam In modern terms the four

championships of the world, which are the US Masters, US Open, British Open and US PGA Championship

Green The putting surface for each individual hole

Greensome Similar to foursomes, except that both players drive and then choose which ball to play

Green fee The amount that one pays to play a game

Gross The number of strokes taken without deduction of handicap

Ground under repair A clearly defined area, by club or committee, from which a player may drop his ball clear without penalty

Gutty A slang term for the original ball made of gutta-percha, which is a rubbery substance obtained from the sap of certain Malayan trees

---

Half or halved A hole is declared to be halved when each side takes the same number of shots. A halved match is drawn

Half shot Less than a full swing

Handicap The method by which any two players can be equally matched in spite of one being better than the other. A player is handicapped by regularly submitting completed scorecards to the club where he is a member

Hanging lie A ball that is on a downward slope so that the player has to over-stretch to play the intended shot

Hazard A general term for bunker, long grass, road, water, whin, molehill, or other bad ground, although in

today's golfing vocabulary it usually refers to a bunker, ditch or pond

Head to head A term used for one player taking on another in an individual match

Heavy Marginally striking the ground behind the ball

Heel The part of the club head nearest the hosel

Hickory A wooden-shafted club, subsequently replaced by steel shafts

Honour The right to play off first from a tee, usually earned by a player scoring less than his opponent on the previous hole

Hooding Pronation of the club head at the address so as to reduce loft and keep the ball lower to the ground

Hook An exaggerated draw – in other words a ball which moves further in the air from right to left than intended by the player

Horseshoed A slang expression for a ball which runs around the cup without going in

Hosel The socket in a club into which the shaft fits

H20'd it A slang expression for hitting a ball into water

In The second nine holes, inward half or as Americans sometimes call it, 'the back side'

Interlocking grip Entwining of the little finger of the right hand with the first finger of the left – or vice versa for a left-hander

Iron A club made of the material which the name implies, with the head more or less laid back to loft the ball. From the number one club to the

	wedge, the iron face becomes larger and more lofted
Jigger	A special club for chipping, or bad lies, now virtually obsolete
Knee-knocker	A slang expression for a particularly tough short putt
Lag	To roll up a putt to a certain holing distance
Lateral water hazard	A natural pond or ditch that runs parallel to the fairway and from where there is a specific procedure within the rules for taking relief
Level (or like) as we lie	When both sides, or both players, have played the same number of strokes
Lie	The situation of the ball on the turf, i.e. a good or bad lie
Lift	To lift the ball is to take advantage of the rules and improve the lie by lifting and dropping the ball, although this might be done at the penalty of a stroke, depending on the circumstances
Line	Intended direction of a stroke
Links	The open downs or heath on which golf is played. Nowadays it usually refers to a seaside course since this is laid out on land referred to as linksland
Lip	Edge of the hole
Loft	To hit the ball so that it arcs through the air; also used for the angle of a club's face by which to achieve this
Loop	A deviation in the path of the swing, the club apparently 'looping' between the completion of the

	backswing and the beginning of the downswing
Long iron	In modern parlance this usually relates to an iron club of number one, two, three or four
Lost ball	A ball is lost if it has not been found within five minutes of beginning a search. It can also be declared lost provided another ball is immediately put into play
Marker	The player responsible for recording another's scorecard
Mashie/ Mashy	An original term for a straight-faced iron-headed club, which would be equivalent to a modern five iron
Match-play	Reckoning the score by holes
Medal play	See *Stroke play*
Menber bounce	A slang expression for good fortune
Metal wood	Misnomer for a club of wooden-headed design, the head in this case being made of metal
Method	Personal style of play
Mixed foursomes	When a man and a woman are partners at foursomes
Municipal course	Known in America as a public course, it is open to anybody on payment of a green fee
Nap	See *Grain*
Net	Player's score after he has deducted his handicap allowance
Niblick	An original term for a small, narrow-headed, heavy iron club used when in a bad lie
Nineteenth	The clubhouse bar, or the first extra play-off hole, when players are all square in match-play after

eighteen holes

On the beach	A slang expression for being in a bunker
Out of bounds	When the ball is struck beyond a boundary which designates the limits of the course
Overlapping grip	Also called the Vardon grip, the little finger of the right hand overlapping the first finger of the left – or vice versa for a left-hander
Out	The first nine holes, outward half or, as Americans sometimes call it, 'the front side'

Par	The theoretical score that a professional is expected to make at a specific hole
PGA	The Professional Golfers' Association
PGA European Tour	The body that organises the professional tour in Europe
Pill	A slang expression for a golf ball
Penalty stroke	This may be added to a player's score under the rules
Pin high	A shot which comes to rest level with the flag, though not necessarily on the green
Pitch	A lofted shot usually executed from out of the rough surrounding a green
Pitch and run	Stroke played with a less lofted club, so that the ball bounces on after landing
Pitching wedge	The implement used for playing a pitch shot
Play club	An original term for a wooden-headed club, with a full-length shaft, more or less supple, with which the ball could be driven to the greatest distance. In modern terms a driver

Playing the like	The playing of a stroke which will equal the number of strokes played by the other side
Playing the odd	The playing of a stroke which will be one more than the number of strokes played by the other side
Play-off	Method of deciding a tie between two or more players in stroke-play. Usually done now by sudden-death (the first player to win a hole) but in the US Open still over eighteen holes
Postage stamp	A small green
Plugged ball	A ball embedded in its own pitch mark
Plus handicap	Handicap allocated to an amateur golfer who regularly scores lower than the standard scratch score
Pot bunker	Small, relatively deep bunker
Preferred lie	Under local rules this will permit a player to improve his lie when on the fairway without incurring a penalty stroke.
Pull	A shot left of the target
Punch shot	To slam the club down into the ball with a short swing so that it keeps the ball low into a wind
Putter	The implement used for strokes on the putting surface
Push	A shot right of the target

Quick	An apparently hurried swing

Rap	A short, sharp putting stroke
Reload	A golfer's expression for taking another ball after hitting the first attempt out of bounds
Rough	Areas adjacent to the

	fairways which are in their natural state, i.e. not mowed	**Square**	with a lofted head so that it would loft the ball When a game stands evenly balanced, i.e. neither side being ahead
Royal and Ancient	The governing body of the game based at St Andrews, Scotland	**Square to square**	A method of teaching wherein the clubhead remains at right angles to the line of play throughout the swing
Rub of the green	A favourable or unfavourable happening for which there is no redress	**Stableford**	A method of scoring in which a player is awarded one point for a score of
Run-up	A low chip shot		one over par at a specific
Rutting iron	Old-fashioned club, now extinct, used for difficult lies		hole; two points for a par; three points for a birdie; four points for an eagle
Sand iron/ sand wedge	A club with a sharp-angled face, usually employed for hitting the ball out of a bunker	**Standard scratch score**	The number of strokes in which a scratch player is expected to complete the course
Sclaff	Scottish term for hitting the ground behind the ball	**Staying down**	Ability not to lift the head before hitting the ball
Shag bag	Practice-ball bag	**Stone dead**	A shot which finishes very
Shank	A mis-hit shot in which the ball is struck with the hosel of the club and flies off at right angles. Also known as a 'socket'	**Stretcher bearer**	close to the hole A slang expression for caddies
Set	A full complement of clubs. A player today may, under the rules, put a maximum of fourteen clubs in his bag	**Stroke index**	Where a handicap golfer receives his handicap strokes, either against another player or against the card
Shaft	The stick or handle of a club	**Stroke holes**	The hole or holes at
Short game	A reference to that part of the game played on or around the putting surface		which, in handicapping, a stroke is given by the better player to the inferior player
Short iron	A term usually applied to an eight, nine or ten club. A ten is a pitching wedge	**Stroke play**	Reckoning the score by strokes
Singles	A game between two players	**Stymie**	An original term, no longer applicable, for when a player's ball lies
Slice	To hit the ball so that it moves violently from left to right through the air		in the line of that of an opponent
Snap hook	A shot that curves violently from right to left through the air	**Sway**	Lateral movement of the head and body during the swing
Sole	The flat bottom of the club head	**Sweet spot**	Centre of mass of the club head, hence the point of
Spoon	An original term for a wooden-headed club		the club face which must contact the ball for optimum effect

Swing	The sweep of the club in hitting the ball
Swing weight	Weight of the club head felt by the golfer when swinging the club; adjustable according to individual preference
Take away	The movement of the hands, arms and club away from the ball
Tee	Originally a pat of sand on which the ball was placed for the first stroke at each hole. Nowadays a tee is made of wood or plastic
Tee marker	The designated spot on a teeing ground on a given day for starting the playing of a hole
Teeing up	The act of placing the ball on a tee to strike the first shot at any given hole
Tempo	As with rhythm, a smooth and unhurried swing
Temporary green	Mostly used in winter and then only in an emergency to save a normal green from damage
Texas wedge	A reference to a putter when it is employed for hitting a shot from off the green or from out of a bunker
Thin	A slight mis-hit resulting from the leading edge of the sole of the club hitting the ball
Threeball	Contested between three players, each in opposition to the other two
Threesome	Two players in partnership, using one ball as in foursomes, against a single player with his own ball
Through the green	Everywhere on the course except on the tee or the green of the hole being played
Tight course	One on which it can be punishing to miss narrow fairways because of heavy rough or thick vegetation
Toe	Part of the club face furthest from the shaft
Top	To hit a ball above its centre
Trap	American expression for bunker
Twitch	See *Yips*
Underclub	To take one, two or more clubs less than those required to enable the ball to reach the desired target
Up	A golfer is up when he has won more holes than his opponent
Upright	A swing in which the arc is closer to a vertical than a horizontal plane
Water hazard	Lake, pond, river, ditch or sea
Wedge	A sharply angled club usually referred to as a pitching wedge or a sand wedge and employed for extracting the ball from a difficult or hazardous lie
Whin	Furze or gorse
Whipping	The pitched twine uniting the head of the club to the handle
Windcheater	A slang expression for a shot that is deliberately struck low so as to keep it under the wind
Wood	A club with a head made of wood such as persimmon
Wry neck	Club in which the head is aligned slightly behind the shaft, most common in putters
Yips	Uncontrollable action on a putter which causes a player consistently to miss short putts

USEFUL ADDRESSES

English Golf Union
1–3 Upper King Street
LEICESTER
LE1 6XF   (0533) 553042

English Ladies' Golf Association
Edgbaston Golf Club
Church Road
BIRMINGHAM
B15 3TB   (021) 456 2088

Irish Golf Union
Glencar House
Eglinton Road
DONNYBROOK
Dublin 4   (0001) 694111

Irish Ladies' Golf Union
1 Clonskeagh Square
Clonskeagh Road
DUBLIN 14   (0001) 696244

Ladies' Golf Union
The Scores
St Andrews
FIFE
KY16 9AT   (0334) 75811

PGA European Tour
Volvo Tour
The Wentworth Club
Wentworth Drive
Virginia Water
SURREY
GU25 4LS   (09904) 2881

Royal and Ancient Golf Club
St Andrews
FIFE   (0334) 72112

Scottish Golf Union
The Cottage
181a Whitehouse Road
Barnton
EDINBURGH
EH4 6BY   (031) 339 7546

Scottish Ladies' Golfing Association
Chacewood
49 Fullarton Drive
TROON
KA10 6EL   (0292) 313047

Welsh Golfing Union
2 Isfryn
Burry Port
DYFED SA16 0BY   (05546) 2595

Welsh Ladies' Golf Union
Ysgoldy Gynt
Llanhennock
Newport
GWENT
NP6 1LT   (0633) 420642

Women Professional Golfers' European
Tour
The Tytherington Club
MACCLESFIELD
CHESHIRE   (0625) 611444